LITTLE
EXERCISE BOOKS
Brain games for personal wellbeing

EXERCISES FOR
LETTING GO

Rosette Poletti & Barbara Dobbs

Illustrations Jean Augagneur

The Five Mile Press

The Five Mile Press Pty Ltd
1 Centre Road, Scoresby
Victoria 3179 Australia
www.fivemile.com.au

This edition published 2012, Reprinted 2012
First published 2008 by
Éditions Jouvence, S.A.
Chemin du Guillon 20
Case 184
CH-1233 Bernex
www.editions-jouvence.com
info@editions-jouvence.com

Cover and page layout: Éditions Jouvence
Cover and internal illustrations: Jean Augagneur
except the illustrations of the mandala (p. 33),
the mazes (pp. 38 and 55) and the lotus flower (p. 51)
reworked or illustrated by Barbara Dobbs.
The flowers are taken from *Les harmonisants émotionnels
du Dr Bach*, Barbara Dobbs, Recto-Verseau, Romont, 2006.
Translated into English by Patsy Abott-Charles
Formatting in English translation: Caz Brown

ISBN: 978 1 74300 260 5

Printed in China

Let go.
How easy it is to say!
But how do you do it?
The aim of this little exercise book is
to suggest ways and practical exercises
to help you to let go.

Do you know how monkeys
are caught in Indonesia?

An orange is put in a
large pumpkin. The monkey
slides his hand inside
and takes the fruit. He
can't retract his hand
because it's holding the
orange and, because he
doesn't want to let go of
it, he's stuck there and is
captured.

What is your orange?
What can't you let go of?

Perhaps you feel resentful — of someone or something.
Or you have a regret.
Or something is stuck in your mind.
A thought that you know is wrong but you just can't
remove from your brain.
Or a feeling of guilt.

4

<u>What prevents you from letting go?</u>

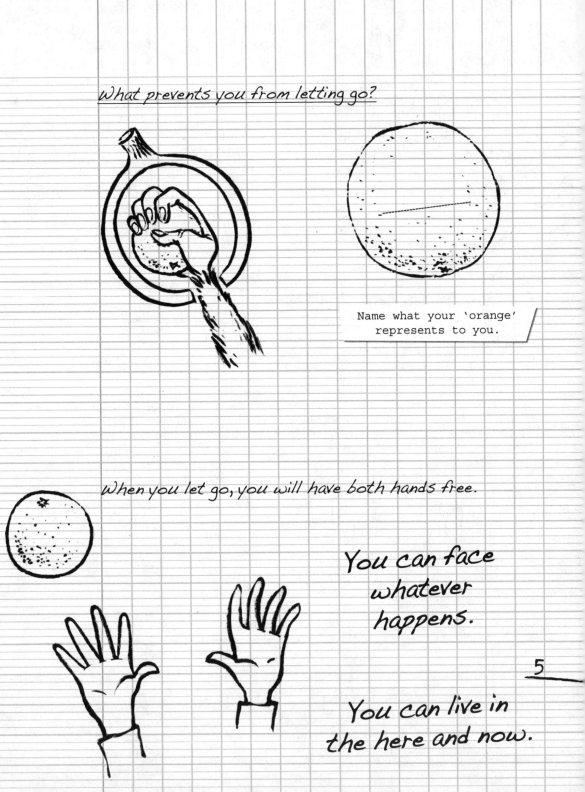

Name what your 'orange' represents to you.

When you let go, you will have both hands free.

You can face whatever happens.

5

You can live in the here and now.

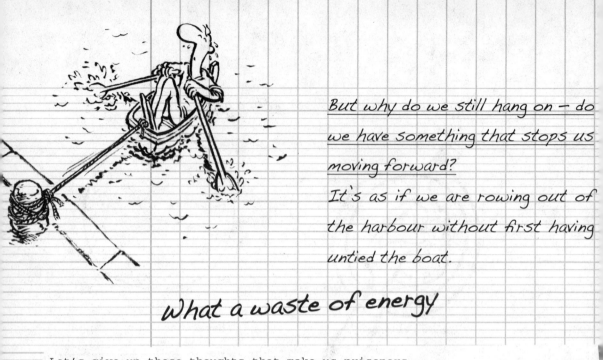

But why do we still hang on — do we have something that stops us moving forward?

It's as if we are rowing out of the harbour without first having untied the boat.

What a waste of energy

Let's give up these thoughts that make us prisoners.
Some of our thoughts create a real prison. We must remove them one by one, as you would cut the bars of a prison window. So, what is it that stops us sawing at these bars, letting go of the orange, untying the boat? Our thoughts, our ideas, have come to us from our parents, our family, our teachers and our guides. They've given us thoughts and ideas that we've absorbed and then enlarged and developed within ourselves to the point where they've become **fixed ideas**.

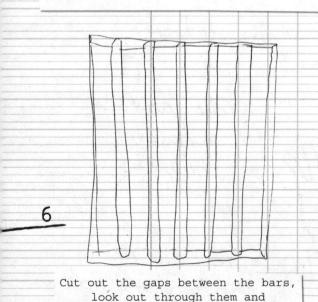

Write your pressures on a piece of fruit or a ball

Cut out the gaps between the bars, look out through them and tear up some of them.

Cut out the circle and 'hold' the pressure.
Feel like the monkey.
Drop the fruit.
You will feel more human.

Like the monkey that doesn't understand that there are other oranges and that he can climb anywhere in the trees to collect them, we have 'accepted' our limiting ideas.

- Life's ridiculous.
- Happiness doesn't exist.
- You feel guilty about not making other people happy — especially your parents, your partner and your children.
- There is only one good solution and you've haven't found it.
- Anyway, what's the point, you'll never make it.

What are these thoughts that have been given to you and you have turned into fixed ideas? Write them down below.

...

...

...

...

...

7

Now, take a red pencil and strike them all out firmly.

Then, across the page, write in green:

'They're false, I no longer believe them!'

Look for an antidote. What is exactly right for you at this moment? Write a positive and helpful sentence for you and your life. For example:

· Life is exciting, fascinating ...
· Every day is a good day to be alive!
· ...
· ...
· ...
· ...
· ...
· ...
· ...
· ...
· ...
· ...
· ...
· ...
· ...
· ...
· ...
· ...

8

Sometimes you feel you are being held back, cornered by other ideas, simple and often subtle, which have not only been said to you but have shown themselves through the behaviour of your family.

They determine your own behaviour; they stick in your mind without you realising it. Here are some examples:

· You have a difficult relationship, a heavy burden from which you no longer get any pleasure. Nonetheless, you continue with it because you've persuaded yourself that it's your duty and you can't change the situation.

You're carrying someone!

Why?
Because you've persuaded yourself that you must be **strong**, <u>9</u> that you must **help** them, but you receive no help in return. And still you go on with it.

· Perhaps you've seen one of your parents or grandparents behave like this? What burden have you seen your father or mother carry? Can you identify it? Can you give it a name?

· What burdens or baggage are you carrying that you don't want to carry any more? Name them.

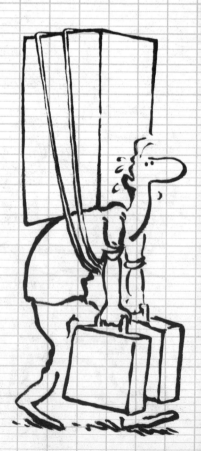

Do you want to change the situation? If the answer is yes, here are two ways to get there:

· Find a big stone. Write on it, using a permanent marker, the name of the burden you no longer wish to carry. Then, throw it in a pond or lake or river, as far out as possible.

It doesn't mean at all that you have rejected a person (if it is a person!) or that you have cut your ties with them. It's simply that you accept that they live their life and that you have the right to live yours!

In his work ATMA, The Power of Love — How to Recover One's Potential in Life, Jacques Martel suggests another way:

On the page opposite, simply draw a picture of yourself and the other person, as shown in the sketch, left.

Then, draw a circle symbolising a ball of shining light around yourself and around the other person, just like in the example, left

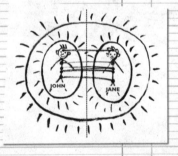

Then, draw a circle of shining light around both the figures, as well as lines linking the figures through their centres of energy, or chakras, as in the example, left.

12

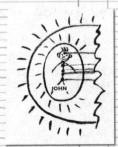

Finally, cut the drawing in half, as shown in the example left.

You don't cut yourself or the person, of course, just the lines of harmful attachment, of the internal prison that the attachment created. This technique is very powerful because it is directed to the subconscious.

Me   Other person

Perhaps you are one of those people who is never satisfied with what they've done, or what they've made or
produced. The 'bad fairy' says:

'Be perfect!'

Since that day, you have never been content with yourself. You've never been satisfied with what you've done
or, worse, you've never dared to create anything. You've
tidied your paintbrushes, sold your guitar and let your
colours dry out. Just because you can't be Vincent van
Gogh, doesn't mean you shouldn't try!

The good fairy now says:

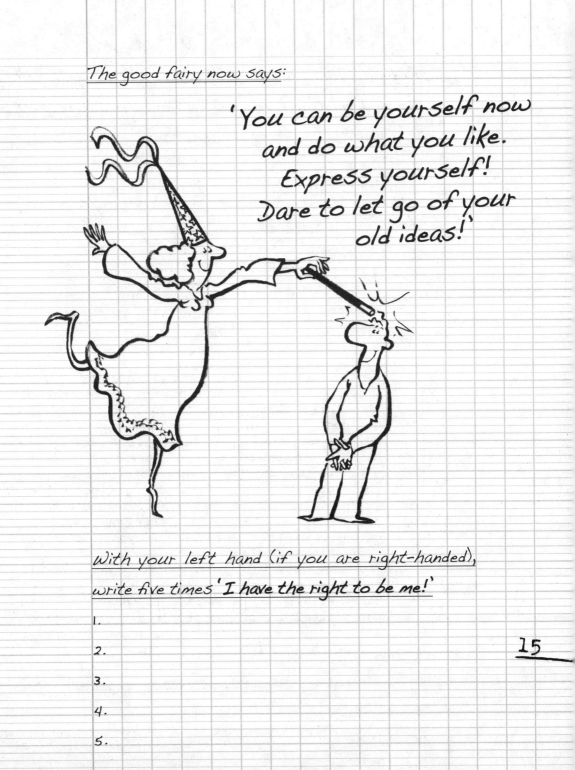

'You can be yourself now
and do what you like.
Express yourself!
Dare to let go of your
old ideas!'

With your left hand (if you are right-handed),
write five times 'I have the right to be me!'

1.

2.

3.

4.

5.

15

And with your right hand (if you're left-handed), write five times 'I'm letting go of waiting for others to respect me'.

1.

2.

3.

4.

5.

Because only you can create the quality of your life. While you aren't always in control of the things that happen to you, it is you who decides what your attitude towards them will be. You may also often feel guilty because you haven't managed to 'please' your family, or to satisfy your boss's demands, or those of your colleagues ... If this is what you believe of yourself, you may have the uncomfortable feeling of not being everything that you should be, of not being able to please everyone, to not be 'all things to all people'.

You know very well that you've given yourself an impossible task, but nevertheless, you continue with it. Abraham Lincoln once said: 'One can please some of the people all of the time, all of the people some of the time, but never all of the people all of the time.'

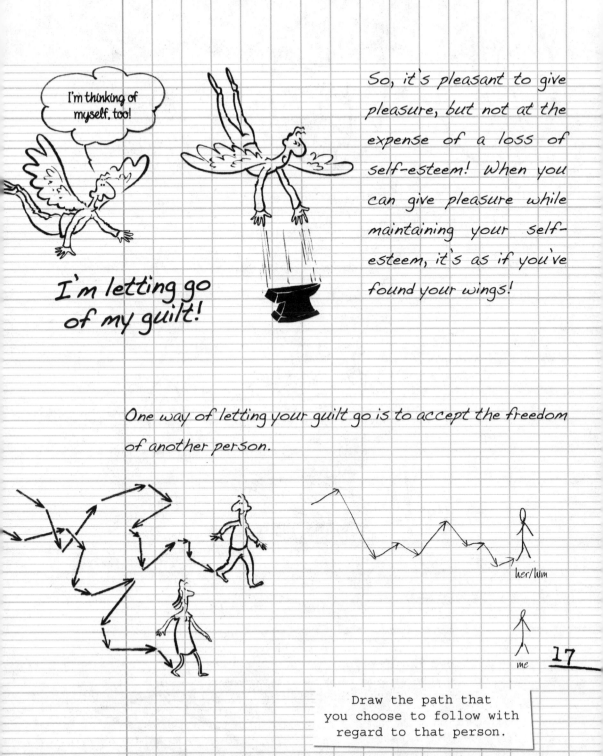

I'm thinking of myself, too!

I'm letting go of my guilt!

So, it's pleasant to give pleasure, but not at the expense of a loss of self-esteem! When you can give pleasure while maintaining your self-esteem, it's as if you've found your wings!

One way of letting your guilt go is to accept the freedom of another person.

her/him

me

17

Draw the path that you choose to follow with regard to that person.

I don't have to live his life!

My space

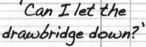
His/her space

I can build bridges, as long as there are drawbridges that guarantee a person's freedom.

'Can I let the drawbridge down?'

'No, not for a moment!'

18

Choose how far you want to let the drawbridge down by tracing over the pen in the relevant position.

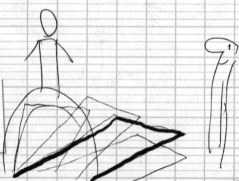

Let go of the hurts that you've suffered

There are several ways of doing this:

- **Review the hurt while asking yourself two questions:**
  1. 'Did the other person really want to hurt me?'
     Spoken words can sound worse than the thoughts behind them. You may have been that person's target, but the internal motives that prompted her to speak in this way were perceived by you as hurtful, betraying, spiteful.
  2. Do you really know the real motivation of other people?

Whether the other person did or did not want to hurt me, I can let go of my hurt through doing the following exercise:

In a calm environment where I am alone, standing well-balanced on my feet, I decide to clear out all the hurts from my heart.

With your right hand on your heart, breathe deeply while letting out an 'Ahah' as loudly as possible. Do this ten or twelve times.

At each exhalation, while you are making the 'Ahah' sound, imagine that you are ridding yourself of all these hurts, removing them from your body.

Then give yourself a few moments of calm, sitting comfortably, and, for a few minutes, reflect on what you've just done.

19

• Use visualisation

Here is another way to let go. It's called *visualisation*, and it's recognised as being very useful **for ridding yourself of negative memories**:
Seat yourself in a comfortable position with your back straight ... Close your eyes ... Concentrate on your breathing ... This is all about becoming aware of things.
On inhalation think to yourself: *'I am breathing in, I feel a calmness ...'* and on exhalation: *'I'm breathing out, I feel good ...'*. You need to repeat this ten times.

Think of a situation, a person, a feeling or a memory that obstructs you, that you've never succeeded in letting go. Identify it exactly: the neighbour's dog that barks in the middle of the night, a colleague who has betrayed you, your son who has given up his studies, difficulties you are having with your mother-in-law ... Think about the things that particularly upset you.

Then, open your eyes, take a piece of paper and illustrate the situation with a very simple drawing.
Write at the bottom of the drawing: **'I refuse to continue sheltering fears, feelings of anger and sadness that come from this situation.'**
Then, using your black pen, enclose the situation carefully in a circle. For a few moments more, and for the last time, envisage the situation in your mind. Then, crumple up the paper and throw it as far as possible from you or, better, burn it. It's a method of 'cutting out' an unhealthy personal attachment connected to that situation. Your subconscious will recognise this symbolic action, and letting go will therefore be easier.

• Find internal peace again

We can feel hurt by an attitude of indifference, of rejection, or by an absence of recognition from people whom we have helped, from those to whom we have devoted or 'sacrificed' ourselves. It's important to remember that a true gift doesn't expect to be repaid, that it's better not to give than to do so hoping for recognition. If you have these sorts of hurts, you can let them go by doing the following **exercise**:

Sitting comfortably and calmly, breathe in and out five or six times. Then say as you inhale: *'I'm breathing in and I feel calm'* and as you exhale: *'I'm breathing out and I feel great!'* Finally, open your hands, palms up, and repeat five times: *'I give and I expect nothing in return.'*

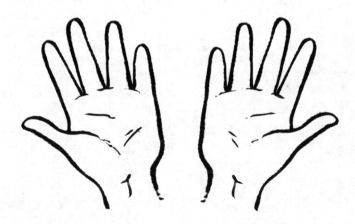

You will immediately feel an enormous calm come over you and from now on, each time you give something to someone, you should repeat: *'I give and I expect nothing in return.'* You will very soon see the results from the calm that flows through you!

• Draw your hurts

You can also let go of a hurt by doing the following exercise:

Draw your hurt. What shape is it? What colour is it? What are its measurements?

Let the answers to these questions come of their own accord. Take your time ...

Then tear the page out and tear it up into tiny pieces, and throw them out or burn them while imagining that your resentment and your hurt are being destroyed too.

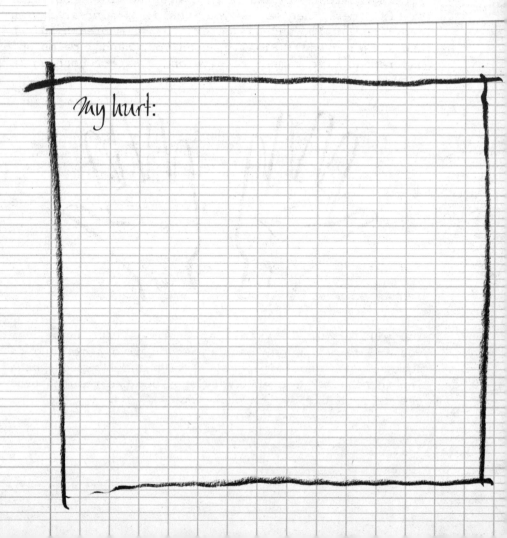

My hurt:

• The gift

Now imagine that you've received a beautifully wrapped parcel with your name on it. You open it and find a letter written on parchment saying the following:

My dear friend,
You've done so well. You've had the courage to let go or start to let go of this sad memory. I've got good news for you. Beneath this problem, beneath the hurt, there was a gift for you: because of what you've endured, you've learned something; you've become more open to yourself and to others. You alone know the nature of this gift, examine it thoroughly and accept it. Then define it below:

What I've discovered from this hurt, this problem, is:

...

...

...

...

I now know that each morning I can say: 'I'm confident that I've let go.

23

• Recover internal serenity

Then, deep in the centre of yourself, you're going to find the need to go even further than letting go; you will be able to go towards ... (find the word in the column below):

```
f e v e r
d e p o s i t
g u i t a r
t r e e
s t r e a m e r
s t a r c h
n e p t u n e
```

Yes, beyond letting go, there is **forgiveness**.

To forgive is not an act of volition; it's a road that develops in the centre of yourself, a road to freedom. It's a possibility, a way of finding serenity in your heart again.

To forgive is to calmly walk along a rocky road where there are stopping points such as:

- Deciding not to take revenge and to stop using offensive words.
- Accepting the fact that you have been hurt.
- Acknowledging what you have lost (for example self-confidence, confidence in another) so that you can mourn the loss.
- Accepting emotions like anger, sadness, fear.
- Starting with forgiving yourself.
- Starting to understand the person who hurt you.
- Making sense of what has happened.
- Turning the page.

Letting go of the need to control others and your surroundings

We all love to control. It's a means of reassuring ourselves and reducing our anxieties. To control someone is to say to them:

- 'You should ...'   - 'I want you to ...'
- 'You have to ...'   - 'You mustn't do ...'

We want to control others; however, we don't like to be controlled ourselves.

First stage:

<u>Who has tried to control you in your life?</u>

Put their names on each figure. Do you still let them control you?

Take a red marker and strike out the lines that connect you to the people who try to control you.

Draw and stick their head here

Draw and stick their head here

'Wow! Freedom's great.

Draw and stick their head here

Draw and stick your head here

Draw and stick their head here

Draw and stick their head here

Draw and stick their head here

Choose some music that you like and have a little dance!

26

Draw your head

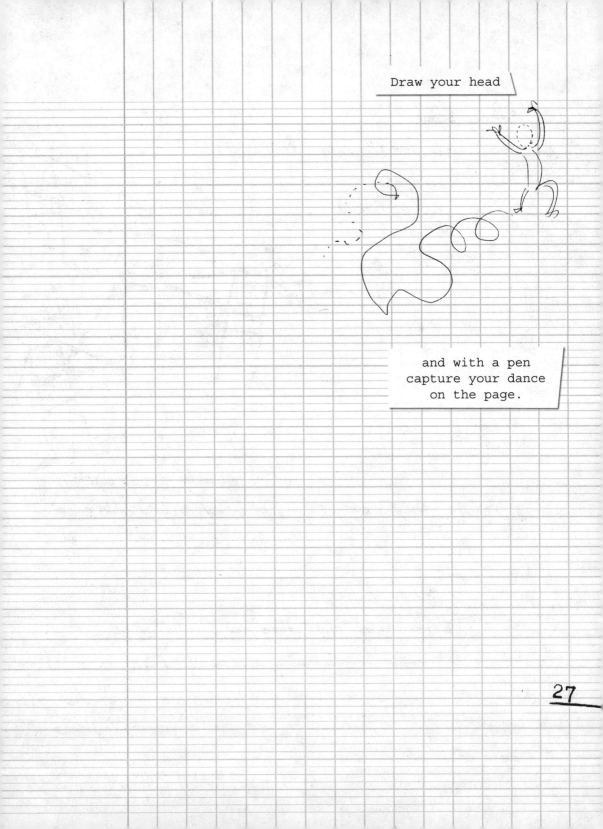

and with a pen
capture your dance
on the page.

Second stage:

Who are the people that you wish

to control?

· in your family:

...

...

...

· at work:

...

...

...

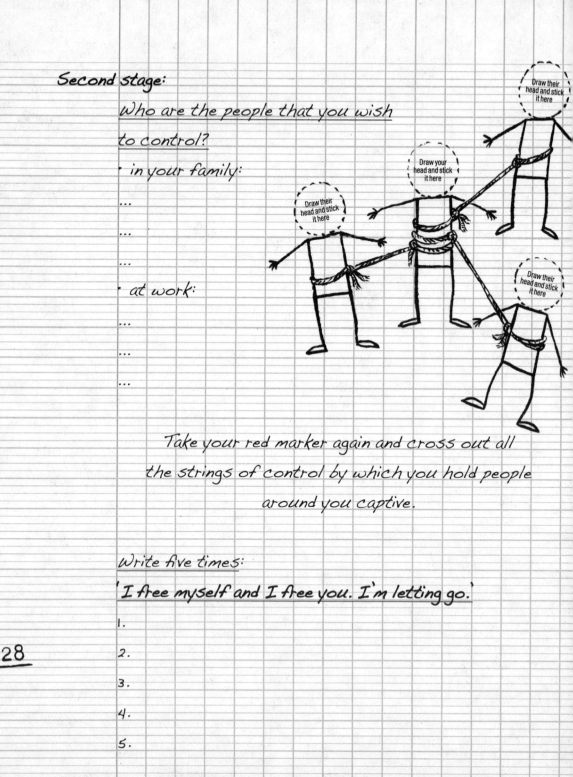

Take your red marker again and cross out all
the strings of control by which you hold people
around you captive.

Write five times:

'I free myself and I free you. I'm letting go.'

1.

2.

3.

4.

5.

28

Letting go of the need to be right

'I'm right!'

How many times a day do you say these words?
Or one of the following versions:
- 'I was certainly right!'
- 'You're wrong!'

If you want to be happy, don't always think you have to be right. Live your life and let others live theirs. If you love them, you owe them freedom. So let go of the need to be right!

To be right

To be wrong

I'm right

I was right

Take a black pen and cross out these words.

You'll see that I'm right

<u>Choose a sentence and try using it instead of speaking of right and wrong!</u>

Can you tell me how you view this?.

That's interesting

I see it differently but thanks for giving your point of view.

Thanks for showing a different viewpoint.

....
....
....

Thanks for sharing your opinion with me.

With a green or pink marker, frame the sentence you like most with little flowers.

Letting go in your daily life

Sometimes it's most difficult to let go in respect of the little annoyances of everyday life:

- Someone pushes in front of you in a queue.
- The sales assistant treats you as if you were an intruder rather than a customer.
- A driver thoughtlessly cuts in.
- You miss your bus.
- Your friend is late.
- A small child cries throughout the plane trip.
- The waiter doesn't understand your order and brings you something you didn't ask for.
- It rains when you want to go out for a walk.

What are you going to do?

...

...

...

What are you going to say?

...

...

...

Oh, you can voice your frustration, let everybody know how you feel, put somebody else in their place, talk about your rights ... but you could let go, decide that peace is better than conflict, that the most important thing in life is not to dwell on these details and that: '*Today is a great day to be alive!*' Letting go is all about just being, it's about concentrating on what is positive, beautiful and good.

32

If you feel that it's difficult for you to return to inner peace, colour the mandala on the next page; it's a sure way of rediscovering the calm inside yourself.

33

Letting go after major hardships: illnesses, separations, bereavements ...

How can we talk about letting go in these hard-to-bear situations? At first you may think it's not possible. However, all human beings look for a good quality of life and the chance to live without suffering.

Since the earliest times, and in all important expressions of worldly wisdom, it's clear that the thing that causes the most suffering to humans is their resistance to reality.

Just take a moment to colour this text below:

resistance is the cause of suffering

34

Then, in the space below, write or draw your reaction
to that sentence:

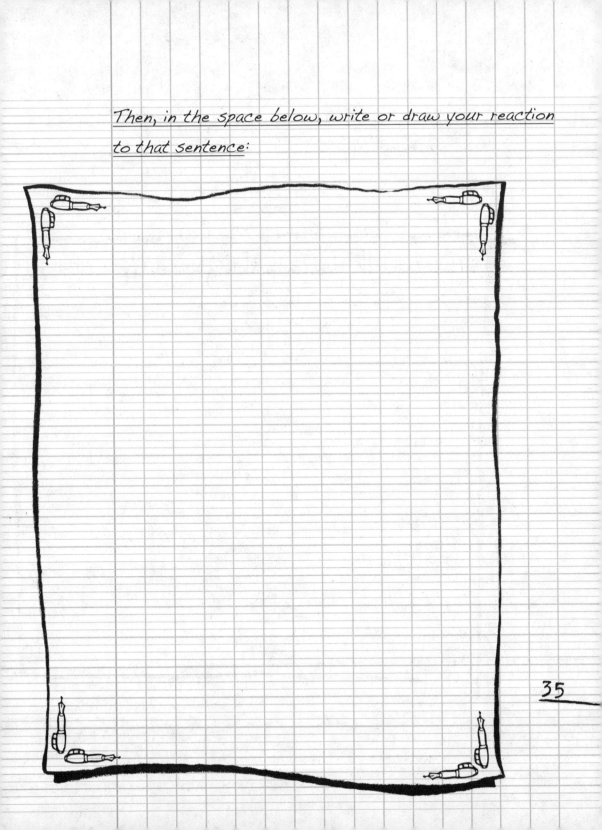

Then identify what is making you suffer at this moment ...

Thing(s) that are making me suffer now:

Do you recognise any resistances there? For example:
'I'm suffering because I haven't been able to have children and I find this unfair. I would have been a good mother and there are plenty of children whose parents haven't really wanted them.'

The resistance here is the non-acceptance of reality.
Yes, it's a terrible disappointment. Yes, it's difficult to live through and that's the reality. Little by little, acknowledgement of your reality provides the solution to inner completeness. It's all about a road, sometimes long, sometimes painful, that becomes a road with no end. Therefore, you must retrace your steps patiently and find the way out. It can be found; it's called *accepting your reality, letting go and discovering serenity.*
You will once again enjoy the spice of life!

37

Using a green pencil, go into the maze and
find the way out:

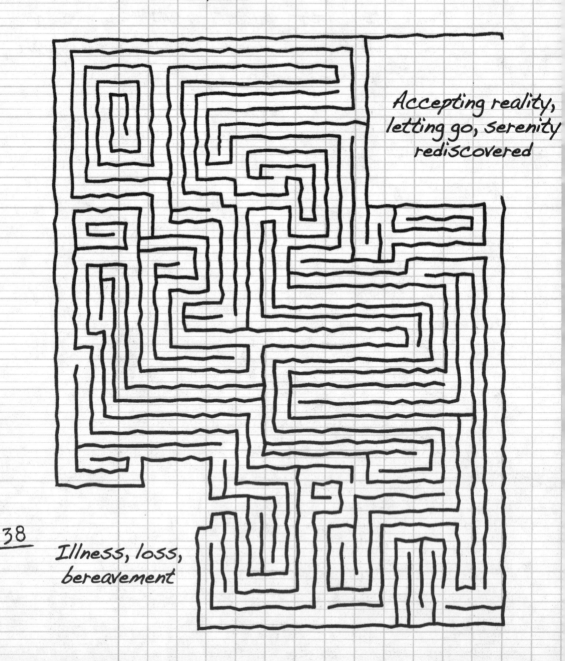

Accepting reality,
letting go, serenity
rediscovered

Illness, loss,
bereavement

Following difficult bereavements (sudden, such as suicides)

Here also is a road that has to be gone down, a road of rebellion, of sadness, of doubts. Then the time comes to turn the page, to keep the memory without suffering, and to hold onto everything that was good and beautiful, to give thanks for everything that we've received from the person who has left us. It's called lifting the 'cloak of mourning' that kept us away from the spice of life.

The time for letting go is now.

I was hidden under the cloak of mourning.

I'm going to rediscover the spice of life!

The person that you loved is there, still present in your heart, but the time has come to live and rediscover the joys your life has given you.

<u>Make a list of eight joys of life that you like the most.</u>

1.   5.

2.   6.

3.   7.

4.   8.

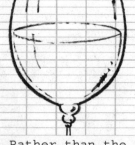

I choose the glass
half full!

Rather than the
glass half empty!

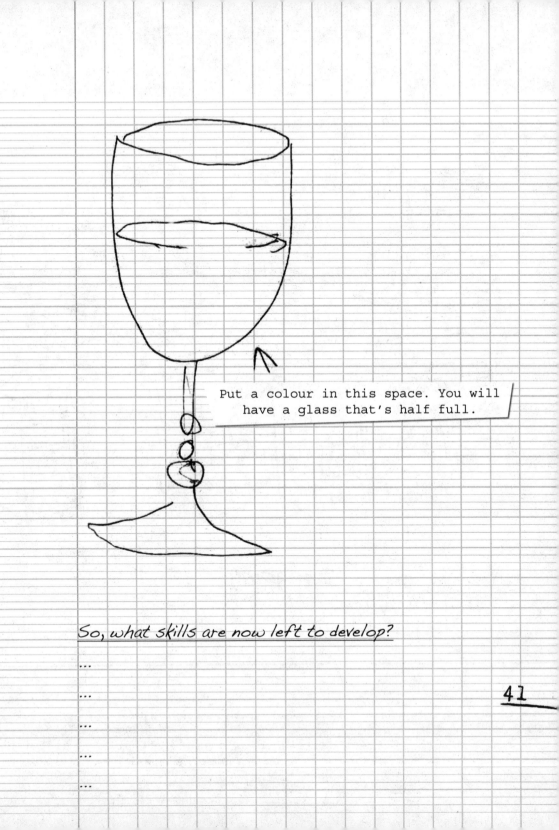

Put a colour in this space. You will
have a glass that's half full.

So, what skills are now left to develop?

...

...

...

...

...

Find the seven mistakes

'I'm going to let go!'

The game of seven mistakes: the answers
1. A drawer is missing.
2. A shoe is missing.
3. 'Very urgent' is written instead of 'urgent'.
4. A pen is missing.
5. An exercise book on the left pile is different.
6. A rose is missing.
7. The eyebrows are missing.

Letting go, letting go ... ???

It sometimes happens that you don't really see what it is that you need to let go of.

You simply feel down, discouraged or sad. Life no longer has the pleasure it used to have, but you don't really know why.

There is a little acronym, which is very helpful and was given to us following a training course in the United States: **FOG**. Fog of course means a cloud of dense mist.

The **F** in fog refers to fear.

What sorts of fears, real or imagined, stop you letting go?

...

...

...

...

...

43

What do these fears do for you? Do you keep them because they are perhaps useful? They prevent you from moving on, from taking risks or from being in disagreement with your family. Only you know what roles these fears play.

My fear of ...

is useful because it protects me from ...

My fear of ...

is useful because it protects me from ...

Do you want to keep them?

O Yes   O No

If yes, for how long?

...

If no, how are you going to protect yourself without them?

...

...

...

...

Let's return to our three letters: **FOG**.

The **O** is the first letter of
the word *obligations*.

You have obligations and you don't want to let go of
them.

Who has put these obligations on you?

...

...

...

Do you often say to yourself: ' I am obliged to ...'?
O Yes   O No

What are your 'real obligations'?

Real obligations:

Note them down
here:

What are these 'obligations' that weigh you down and which you'd like to let go?

· In your family life?

Family life:

· In your business or professional life?

Business or professional life:

- *In your personal life?*

Personal life:

- *In your social life?*

Social life:

47

• In your spiritual life?

Spiritual life:

What makes you take on these obligations?

...

...

...

Now you have made the decision to take a careful look at all these obligations and to keep only those that are absolutely necessary, and/or that correspond with the person you really are.

48

Take a red pencil and cross out all the obligations that you can remove. Was it difficult? Did something hold you back?

Here's the last of the three letters of the word **FOG**.

The **G** of guilt, which indicates 'culpability'.

Why are you living with these fears and why do you accept these unnecessary obligations? Because if you let them all go, you're going to feel guilty.

- Guilty of not being everything to everyone.
- Guilty of not being able to make your own decisions, instead always doing what your parents decided for you.
- Guilty of being the cause of annoyance to someone.

Guilt is the no. 1 enemy of letting go!

Your letting go of your fears and obligations may well not suit some of your family or friends.

If you let go of those obligations that you have crossed out in red, who among your circles of family, friends and acquaintances will make you feel guilty?

...

...

...

...

For what reasons?

...

...

...

...

Is it justifiable that your fears, obligations and guilt always make you feel uncomfortable?

Don't answer that immediately. Take time to put on some gentle music that you like, make yourself comfortable in a nice place with a box of coloured pencils, and give yourself a moment of quiet positive meditation while colouring the lotus flower on the page opposite. While you're doing this, let your mind ponder the question above.

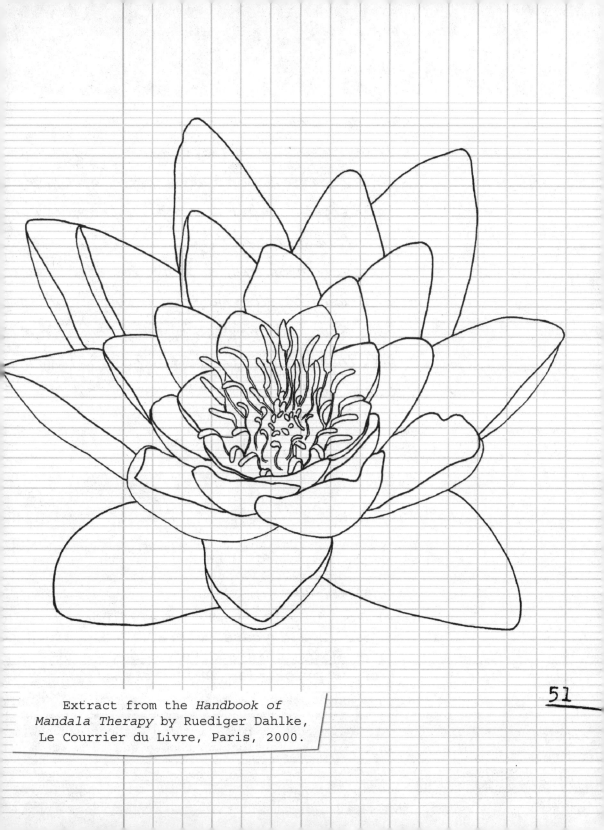

Extract from the *Handbook of Mandala Therapy* by Ruediger Dahlke, Le Courrier du Livre, Paris, 2000.

Now you probably have your answer.

- If you've answered 'Yes, I'm keeping my obligations because I don't want to feel guilty', you haven't yet reached the stage when you can move forward to letting go.

- If you've answered 'No, this feeling of guilt isn't going to stop me from letting go of the obligations and unnecessary fears that ruin my life', then it's time to decide what you're going to say and to whom.

It is possible to say no and to disengage yourself, with kindness and confidence, from obligations that weigh on you. It can be done verbally or in writing, depending on the circumstances. For example:

> 'After spending ten years as a voluntary child-minder in a daycare centre, I've decided to stop doing this and turn myself to other priorities in my life.'

The essential point when someone wants to undo certain obligations is first to have made that decision, then to express it in a way that is both firm and without excuses. Every human being has the right to choose and to make decisions on the basis of those choices.

Letting go of obligations that weigh you down will bring about a wonderful feeling of freedom. However, it may not always be comfortable, certainly not at the beginning, because people who have benefitted from your involvement won't always readily accept losing what you have given them. This is the moment when it is necessary to understand completely that everything the other person says only concerns him or her, and does not take you into account. For example:

'I'm very surprised that a person like you, with the time and the skills, is giving up helping at the daycare centre which depends on volunteers. You ought to think of the overworked parents who need to leave their children in our care.'

What is your reply?

...

...

...

...

53

Listen but don't let it get to you; say:

'I understand your surprise but in fact
I have decided to use my time and my
efforts for other priorities.'

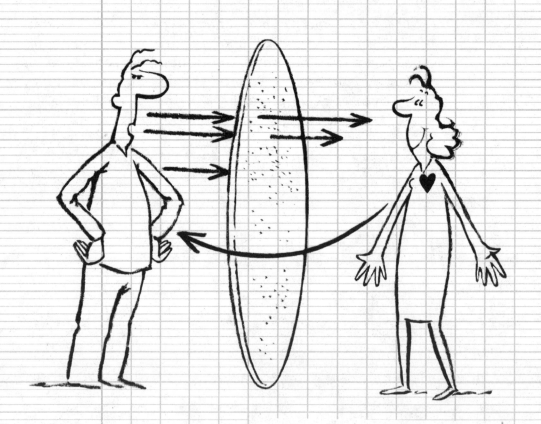

The filter that allows me
to listen to another without
feeling moved by negative
emotions.

To let go is to rediscover what's essential

To let go of fears, unnecessary obligations and guilt is of enormous benefit. It opens the possibility of acquiring much greater internal peace and serenity. It also reduces stress, anxiety and disappointment.

Letting go enables you to clear out the inessentials in your life, to rediscover yourself and what your essentials are.

Rediscover the essential: human beings have always pursued this quest. One of the most beautiful symbols of it is the maze of the cathedral of Notre-Dame at Chartres, which dates from the thirteenth century.

We suggest that you 'walk' though the maze with a coloured pencil, letting yourself meditate on what is 'essential' and what it represents for you.

55

Happiness is internal freedom!

It's the ability to let go.
At the end of your walk through the maze, we suggest the following exercise as a means of evaluating yourself:

1. When I hear the expression letting go, I think of:
...

...

...

2. For me, the essential part of letting go is:
...

...

...

3. I understand that I can move towards this by:
...

...

...

4. Difficulties that I could encounter in my journey towards letting go are:

...

...

...

5. My necessary resources for achieving internal freedom are:

...

...

...

6. What I will gain from letting go of the things I have identified is:

...

...

...

7. Today, I'm going to start with:

...

...

...

Cut out the following positive sentences and choose one of them every day.

Today I accept reality	Today I forgive	Today I let go of my resistances
Today I have confidence	Today I thank someone	Today I let go of a doubt
Today I adapt myself	Today I'm prepared for whatever comes	Today I'm saying yes
Today I don't blame anybody	Today I get rid of clutter in my life	Today I give myself new freedom
Today I let go of an unnecessary rule	Today I accept that I'm not perfect	Today I give without expecting something in return
Today I'm concentrating on love	Today is a wonderful day to be alive	Today is the only day that counts

I've now let go of all the following matters. Write them in the sacks being thrown into the sea below.

I'm free, I say YES to LIFE!

Letting go

Letting go doesn't mean you stop being concerned with other people; it's simply knowing that other people are separate from you and have their own lives.

Letting go doesn't mean you cut yourself off from others; it's simply giving up trying to control them.

Letting go doesn't mean you become indifferent or egotistic; it's accepting that you concern yourself with what belongs to you.

Letting go means accepting that you're not all-powerful and the consequences of your actions aren't solely down to you.

Letting go means accepting reality, even when it doesn't match up with what you want.

Letting go means not dwelling on the past and dreading the future, but living fully and completely in the present.

Letting go means you fear less and love more.

61

Fill this page with as many hearts
as you can.

In conclusion

We hope that by the end of these enjoyable and inter-
active exercises, you've been able to increase your
understanding of the concept of letting go.

By way of ending this little book of exercises, because
there isn't any conclusion to making your personal
decision to let go, we would like to leave you with this
thought so that it may help to remind you in the days
and months to come:

'The ability to let go,
the ability to have
confidence, to adapt
yourself positively, to
assume responsibility for
making sense of your life at
any moment, is to be ready
to say YES, to accept life
and everything that
comes with it!'

To each of you, our readers, we wish you serenity and the joy of living.

Rosette Poletti and Barbara Dobbs

Rosette Poletti and **Barbara Dobbs** are health professionals, nursing specialists and teachers of health and related issues.